GRANDPA'S ENIGMA

GRANDPA'S ENIGMA

✦

A Personal Observation of ADHD from Birth to Teenage

James A Brink
and
Kathy A Leos

iUniverse, Inc.
New York Lincoln Shanghai

GRANDPA'S ENIGMA
A Personal Observation of ADHD from Birth to Teenage

Copyright © 2005 by James Brink

iUniverse books may be ordered through booksellers or by contacting:

iUniverse
2021 Pine Lake Road, Suite 100
Lincoln, NE 68512
www.iuniverse.com
1-800-Authors (1-800-288-4677)

ISBN-13: 978-0-595-34901-2 (pbk)
ISBN-13: 978-0-595-79617-5 (ebk)
ISBN-10: 0-595-34901-3 (pbk)
ISBN-10: 0-595-79617-6 (ebk)

Printed in the United States of America

For Alex, who graciously allowed us to write and publish these stories about him. As he said, "You might just as well, my mom will tell everyone anyway."

Contents

—ACKNOWLEDGEMENT—

Many thanks to Mrs. Mary Jane Schnorf who corrected many of our mistakes, offered suggestions for organizing the chapters, and provided encouragement throughout.

Foreword

I am the father of nine children. I have sixteen grandchildren and three great grandchildren. After forty-nine years of marriage, my good wife Sally died of cancer in 1999.

My oldest daughter, Janet, lives with me. Also, another daughter, Kathy, with her husband Fernando and two children live with me.

The children's names are Jessica and Alexander. Jessica is fourteen and Alex is thirteen. They cannot stand one another. In fact, if asked, Jessica will deny even having a brother. She will, however, vigorously defend him against anyone teasing him or trying to pick a fight with him.

Alex has Attention Deficit Hyperactivity Disorder (ADHD). Although he does well in school, due in large part to the assistance he receives at home from his mother, I believe his condition prompts some teasing from his fellow students. His ADHD, however, also has a plus side. It contributes to the tremendous pleasure he gives to us his family, and to others he comes in contact with.

In this writing, I will attempt to share with you the humor that Alex, almost entirely inadvertently, has shared with us. If I succeed, you will have some good laughs; if not, it will be my fault, not Alex's.

2004
<u>My Family is a Beach</u>

My Mother is the sun that keeps
Me warm and relaxed.

My Father is the tide that goes out to work
And comes back to support our family.

My Sister Jessica is the seashell
Who looks pretty but has sharp edges.

My Grandpa is the ocean floor, deep,
And has seen many things

I am the surfboard who likes to ride the waves
Coming back to shore a little more worn out
Than when I went out.

Alexander Leos
March, 2004
Age 13

1990
San Diego, California

Alexander James Leos (Lay-ose) was born on 16 November 1990. The birth was not easy; neither for Alex nor his mother. Kathy suffered from toxemia so it was decided that she should give birth three weeks prior to the expected date. Her pre-natal doctor had recommended a Caesarean birth; however, he was not present when she entered the hospital. The attending doctor decided to induce labor.

The birth did not go well. The umbilical cord became squeezed causing Alex to be deprived of oxygen for some period of time. Alex had to be pulled from the birth canal by one arm and he suffered a dislocated arm in the process. He was also quite blue and he didn't cry for, what seemed to Kathy, a very long time.

Alex was put in an incubator until his color improved and he was subsequently given therapy for his dislocated arm. The therapy continued at home and amounted to gently rotating his arm. The biggest problem was inserting his arm into the sleeve of a shirt or jacket.

The doctor advised that the oxygen deprivation might cause a learning disability; however, this could not be determined until later, when he is in school. Is the ADHD a result of the oxygen deprivation? Being an engineer, and not a doctor, I have no idea; however, I think it's an interesting thought.

Alex weighed-in at 6 lbs 11 oz and was 20 inches long. The doctor also said that if the birth had taken place one week later, Alex would not have survived. (Because of his increased size, I suppose.)

Memories

In 1990, when Alex was born, my wife Sally and I lived in Gales Ferry, Connecticut. We moved there from San Diego in 1980. The early events in Alexander's life were therefore not observed by me but are rather the vivid recollections of his mother, Kathy.

It seems to me that mothers' memories are incredible when it comes to their children. They often link important world events to the birth of a child or an event in their child's life. They will say things like, "Oh, I remember the day the Korean War started. That was the day little Billy got his first tooth."

Kathy is no exception. She has an indelible memory of the events in her children's lives. She is also an excellent mimic. I am therefore treated, not only to the telling of a story, but also to a visual drama.

Writing about these events is therefore relatively simple. Kathy tells me the story; I merely record it.

The First Year

Alex was a beautiful baby. (I hasten to add that all my children, their children, and my great grandchildren were beautiful babies. You never know who might read this.) Alex had pitch-black hair and a complexion that many would call olive. I prefer to describe Alex as Hispanic looking. He is a multi-racial mix of Irish, English, Spanish, Danish, Basque, Cherokee, Mayan, and Aztec. (A little Norwegian and Apache are probable.) He is definitely not like any of the children that I grew up with in Minnesota in the 1930's and 1940's; although, he was probably not so unique in 1990 San Diego.

Alex was a good baby, a great baby, a perfect baby...for two, wonderful weeks. After that, "He was a nightmare," according to Kathy. He cried incessantly. In order to quiet him, he had to be held, patted, and rocked constantly. Kathy says that this is common with ADHD children. He also banged his head on the crib to get attention. Kathy has learned a lot about ADHD over the years. In truth, she probably knows more about ADHD than she ever wanted to know.

Alex was no better when taken outside. He didn't like the sun, the wind, or the temperature. (In San Diego?) He preferred to cry inside while tightly bundled up. Also, about this time, his nose started to run continuously.

The constant crying was annoying to all of them; especially, Jessica. Living in a mobile home, intensified the annoyance.

One day, when Alex was two-months old, Kathy went to the kitchen to get Alex a bottle. While she was gone, Jessica (Now 15-months old) went to where Alex was lying on the floor, turned him over onto his stomach, and lifted his shirt to remove his batteries. She was no doubt surprised to learn that Alex did not work the same as her baby doll. Kathy says that this was not all that funny at the time.

Fernando's parents had provided a double stroller for them shortly after Alex was born. Jessica sat in front and Alex in the back. At about nine-months of age, Alex would grab Jessica's ponytail, pull her back, bite her neck or her back, and then laugh at the ensuing scream. When disciplined with a two-finger, slap to the lips, Alex would look puzzled that he was being punished for having done such an obviously good thing.

Jessica started calling Alex "Tu Tu". For a long time, no one could figure out why. Fernando was in the habit of saying, "Hi little dude" to Alex each day when he got home from work. One day Jessica, who was standing nearby, immediately followed Fernando's greeting to Alex with, "Hi Tu Tu". Mystery solved!

Jessica soon became a difficult prey for Alex's teeth. She gave his crib and play area a wide berth and kept her eyes on him whenever he was near. She also warned others, which must have frustrated Alex immensely.

And so, we have Alex: growing normally, crying much less frequently, biting no more, but nose still running. In about two weeks, he will attempt the feat that we now take for granted but actually took thousands of years to master. Alex will attempt to walk upright.

1991
Mobility and Speech

Alex had considerable difficulty learning to walk. He was always running into things and he fell frequently. In retrospect, Kathy thinks walking was merely an intermediate goal. What he really wanted to do was run. And run he did! As soon as he was able, he ran at all times, mostly, in the mobile home.

His first words were, "Mama" and "Uh oh" (When he dropped something.) When Kathy would leave him in Fernando's care, he would cry and say, "Mama". Fernando would say, "Sorry mijo, I am not the Mama." Alex's favorite show at the time was called "Dinosaurs" and the baby dinosaur would always say "Not the Mama" anytime the father would try to take care of him.

When accompanying Kathy shopping, Alex had to wear a harness with a leash for his own safety. One day, a woman said to Kathy, "If you loved that child, you wouldn't have a leash on him, like some animal." Kathy said, "It's because I love him that I protect him from running into the street." (I think I would have said something harsher.)

It occurs to me that I have not seen a child in harness for quite some time. One reason may be that, except for occasional trips to the Home Depot or Lowe's, I don't go shopping. My frequent trips to the drug store, I don't consider shopping; just a means of keeping the drug manufactures in business. A second reason, I believe, may be because most shopping is now done in shopping malls rather than the "Downtown", on-street stores that I fondly remember. In the malls, it is still possible to get run over; however, it would more likely be by a sale-crazed shopper than by an automobile. Even in malls, Alex would need a harness in order to keep him from getting lost.

In addition to Alex's new running skill, his nose continued to run. He was frequently congested. When taken for an examination, the doctor said that Alex had allergies.

"To what?" Kathy asked.

"Just about everything," the doctor said. Actually, Alex's doctor was not far off. Alex has since been diagnosed with chronic asthma.

The doctor's answer reminds me of another of my grandsons. He didn't want the light turned off in his bedroom. When his dad asked him what he was afraid of, he said, "Just about everything."

That lad is now serving as a Hospital Corpsman in the U.S. Navy. I have confidence that he will do well in that profession; he already seems to have the vocabulary down pat.

Speaking of vocabulary, Alex's vocabulary now included the all-important words: "mulk", "juice", and "amee" (i.e., "yummy", meaning sandwich.)

At the age of two, Alex composed his first complete sentence. It happened when Kathy dropped a raw egg on the kitchen floor where it made quite a mess, as you can certainly imagine. Alex looked at it and attempted to say, "Oh Mama, that's disgusting." When he said it, however, it sounded like one word, "Ohmamathadegusting." Kathy was, and still is, in the habit of saying, "That's disgusting."

Alex drank a lot of "mulk" and ate a lot of "amees". By the time he was three, he was big, stocky, and strong. When he was excited, which was often, he would run at his mother at full speed. Kathy, if sitting, would raise her foot and both arms in order to counter the charge. Although Alex just wanted some loving, it was the kind of loving a free-safety might bestow on a wide receiver in the NFL. Actually, if Alex plays football, he will more likely be a defensive guard rather than a safety. He has the stocky build of a guard and lacks the speed required of a defensive back.

When Alex was 3, the family moved to a duplex in Chula Vista (A city adjacent to San Diego), having lost the mobile home due to financial difficulties.

1993
The Duplex

The duplex unit that the family moved into was owned by Fernando's parents. Fernando and Kathy had lived there briefly before, when they were first married. It was barely adequate for a family of four. It was very small and consisted of only one bedroom, one bath, a small living room and a small kitchen. The duplex was unfurnished. The family's limited furniture and appliances were moved to the duplex by Fernando and his brothers. A major advantage of living there was that the rent could be late without fear of eviction.

There was a small bed and a sofa bed in the living room. The children were expected to sleep there. From the beginning, this plan was doomed to fail.

Even before Alex was born, while still living in the mobile home, Jessica would cry continuously until Kathy would lift her from her crib and allow her to join her parent's bed. Kathy would come to regret that accommodation.

When Jessica was about thirteen-months old, she could climb out of her crib, drop herself to the floor, and join her parents in their bed. She accomplished the climb by stepping on the padding at the side of the crib, putting her legs over the crib rail one at a time, holding the crib rail tightly with both hands and, after dangling in that position momentarily, drop to the floor. She didn't always land on her feet; in fact, she most often ended up on her backside. After discovering how she managed this somewhat dangerous feat, Kathy resumed lifting her from her crib and taking her to her parent's bed. It would be quite some time before she would be willing to give up the habit of sleeping with her parents.

Although Jessica managed to exit her crib, she never learned to "Escape" from her playpen. (Maybe, she didn't want to.) Another possibility is that, the crib padding which she used as a step to exit the crib, was replaced with webbing in the playpen and she had no step to get to the rail.

Now, in the duplex, both Jessica and Alex (following her lead), refused to sleep in the living room. This, as you might guess, or as Alex would say, "Uh oh", created several problems for Kathy and Fernando.

Sometimes, the children would fall asleep in the living room and Kathy and Fernando would go to their bedroom. After a short while, however, the children would perform their nightly migration to "their" bedroom. The family was lucky (at least partly so) that they had a queen-size bed.

They lived in the duplex for about a year, and then moved to a small apartment in San Diego.

1994
San Diego, California
<u>The Apartment</u>

In 1994, the family moved into the apartment in San Diego. Alex was three at the time, and Jessica was four. It didn't take long for the first problem to develop.

Fernando had gone to work at the shipyard and Kathy was busy unpacking boxes and putting things away. The children were running through the apartment, chasing each other. Alex ran into an open closet and Jessica closed the door after him.

Kathy stopped unpacking to open the closet door and intended to tell them both to settle down and stop running. To her horror, however, the closet door would not open. Apparently, it was locked from the inside. Alex started to cry and Kathy began to panic. She didn't have any tools to force open, or remove the door. After telling Alex, "Mommy will get you out in just a minute," Kathy grabbed Jessica and went to the apartment next door.

A man answered her frantic knock at the door and, when Kathy hurriedly explained the problem to him, the expression on his face (or lack thereof) indicated that he either didn't understand her, or he was unwilling to help her.

In desperation, Kathy repeated the problem using Spanish. He then obviously understood and quickly grabbed a small toolbox and followed Kathy and Jessica back to their apartment.

Using a screwdriver, the neighbor removed the doorknob and disengaged the locking mechanism. Looking at the entire doorknob unit, which he now held in his hands, he said, "Que pendejos!" (Loosely translated-What stupid idiots).

The doorknob was of a type one often find's on bathroom doors that have a push-button lock on the inside. The ones that I am familiar with, however, have a small hole in the outer knob and can be unlocked by inserting a nail or other small, pointed object.

Apartment dwellers, as well as homeowners, often make do with available, but inappropriate repair or replacement parts, and I'm sure that's how the doorknob got installed.

Alex was relieved but very upset when Kathy reached him, picked him up, and gave him a hug. He did, however, stop crying long enough to beg Kathy to give Jessica a spanking for closing the door on him.

For the next two years, Alex would not close any door; not even the bathroom door, and he refused to stay in any room that did not have an open door.

Fernando delivered a six-pack of beer to the helpful neighbor and thanked him profusely.

The apartment had two bedrooms; however, that did not alleviate the sleeping problems. No matter where the children fell asleep, one, or both, would be in bed with the parents before morning.

Although the apartment was closer to the shipyard where Fernando worked, so that he could ride his bicycle to work and leave the car for Kathy, neither of them liked the neighborhood and they only stayed there about six months.

(As I write this, I cannot help but wonder if the frequent moves created some insecurity in the children. I said to Kathy, "Maybe they slept with you because they were afraid you might move out in the middle of the night and leave them behind." More likely, I think it was because of the ingrained habit that began with Jessica.)

1994
Chula Vista
<u>The Migration</u>

I have used the word "Migration" to describe the nocturnal wanderings of Alex and Jessica. There was, however, a larger, family migration occurring.

Our oldest son Jim, a naval officer, was stationed in Norfolk, Virginia and lived in Chesapeake. Our daughters Joanne and Karen, with their families, moved from San Diego to Chesapeake in 1992 and 1994. They were soon joined by our daughter Susan, who moved there from Bridgeport, Connecticut. In 1994, Sally and I left Gales Ferry, Connecticut and moved to Chesapeake; me, somewhat reluctantly because I loved Connecticut. We had lived there ten years, had good friends there, and it reminded me somewhat of Minnesota.

These moves, as well as those that followed, were supported (and suggested) by Sally. I'm convinced that she had a plan to bring the entire family together, and eventually that would happen; thankfully, not in one house, as when they were young.

Our son George decided to move to Chesapeake in 1994. He was renting a condominium on "D" Street in Chula Vista. When he left for Virginia, the Leos family moved into the condominium. Jessica was five at the time, and Alex was four.

The Fight

The condominium was a two-story unit with two bedrooms, two bathrooms (Actually, one was a half-bathroom), a living room and a kitchen. There was no real backyard, just a small, concrete area where the kids could play. The play-area was fenced and had a gate that Kathy kept locked.

One day, a boy who lived nearby, came to the house to play with Alex and Jessica. He was nine-years old and Kathy thinks he must have been bored playing by himself. Although Kathy thought he might be too old to be playing with her children, she unlocked the gate to let him in, and then re-locked the gate.

The children were playing with toys in the play area when, after a short time, Alex started to cry. Kathy went out to check on him.

What she found was Jessica punching and kicking the neighbor boy. As she was pummeling him, she was yelling, "Don't hit my brother!"

The boy was trying to escape Jessica's fury by climbing over the fence. Kathy grabbed Jessica, and when she did, the boy managed to get over the fence.

After allowing some time for Jessica and Alex to settle down, Kathy walked them both to the boy's home to see if he was okay.

The boy's father answered Kathy's knock on the door. Kathy introduced herself and asked if his son was alright. He said, "Yes. Who beat up my son?"

Kathy pointed to Jessica. He looked down at her and then up at Kathy. In somewhat of a shock, he said, "That little girl beat up my son?"

Kathy said, "Yes, and I'm very sorry. She was defending her little, four-year old brother."

The boy's father said that his son got what he deserved for hitting a four-year old boy.

Kathy said that, prior to that incident, she had never seen Jessica behave aggressively.

The Hill

A short time after moving to the condominium, Fernando and Kathy experienced further financial problems and their car was repossessed.

I should point out that Fernando is a skilled welder and pipe fitter and an exceptionally hard worker. His work was primarily in the local San Diego shipyards. Shipyard work was, however, sometimes sporadic and often resulted in layoffs. When he was working, he borrowed his mother's car to get to and from work.

The family only asked us for financial help when they were in desperate need. When they did, Sally would ask me how much we should send them. When I gave her a figure, she usually doubled it and we sent it. (I thought about giving her a low-ball figure; however, she was much too smart for that ploy. Well, at least I had an input to the decision.)

As Jessica was now five-years old, she started kindergarten. There was a long, and rather steep hill between the condominium and Jessica's school-bus stop. Each school day, Kathy, Jessica, and Alex had to walk that hill. Jessica didn't mind because she liked school so much. Kathy didn't like the hill, even though it was, no doubt, good exercise. Alex didn't just dislike the hill, he hated it.

Alex complained the entire ascent of the hill. Many times he would just sit on the sidewalk and refuse to get up and walk.

Kathy would say, "Okay. Come on Jessica. Bye Alex."

After Kathy and Jessica walked a few steps, Alex would get up and yell, "Wait."

Jessica would look back and say, "Come on Alex."

Kathy would tell her not to look back at him but just keep walking. Alex would always follow some distance back complaining, whining, stomping his feet, and going through his sit-and-rise routine.

Lonesome

School provided the first real separation of Alex and Jessica.

Alex often played upstairs in his and Jessica's room while Jessica was in kindergarten. One day, he called down to Kathy and said, "Mama, is Jesse still in school?"

"Yes," Kathy said.

Alex then asked, "Are we lonely?"

Kathy answered, "No. We are not lonely; we're together."

Alex said, "Okay," and went back to playing with his toys. Kathy then realized that Alex missed Jessica, and was in fact, lonely.

Later in the year, before Jessica completed kindergarten, Fernando and Kathy bought a high-mileage, Oldsmobile Toronado from a college student. The student was asking $800 for the car but when he saw the two children, he lowered the price to $600. The car proved to be very reliable. They drove it until they left San Diego, about a year later. It was still running well at that time and they sold it for $600.

"I Do Nothing"

At age four, Alex still preferred to play indoors rather than outdoors in the limited play area. When he played, he was usually noisy, making various dinosaur sounds when playing with his dinosaur figures, and battle sounds when playing with his toy soldiers.

The noises Alex made were actually comforting and reassuring to Kathy. When Alex was quiet, however, it was like a "red flag" to Kathy.

She would call to him, "Alexander James!"

His reply would invariably be, "I do nothing."

That reply was a second "red flag" that would prompt Kathy to immediately go upstairs to check on him.

(I believe that most children know that when their mother uses both their first and middle names, they are suspected of wrongdoing. Alex was apparently no exception to this knowledge.)

One day, when Jessica returned from school, she went upstairs to play and immediately screamed, "Mama! Look what Alex did!"

When Kathy rushed upstairs, Jessica was holding a jumbled mass of "Barbie" dolls, tied together with shoestrings, and one had no head.

Kathy asked Alex, "Why did you do that?"

"They were hostages," Alex said.

Kathy decided that he was watching way-too-much TV.

Even though Alex seemed to prefer to play indoors, he did often play outside. Kathy, however, did not let him play in the dirt. A doctor recently told Kathy that restricting his play that way probably contributed to his allergies because he didn't develop the usual immunities that children develop from such play.

The Poison Hotline

✦

(Alex four-years old, Jessica five)

One day, Kathy decided to give Jessica and Alex some milk and cookies to keep them busy while she went to the garage to remove clothes from the dryer. The children were sitting in their little chairs in the kitchen.

Next to the kitchen, was a small bathroom. Because the toilet there frequently clogged and overflowed, Kathy kept a small plunger next to it.

When Kathy returned from the garage, she found that Alex had emptied his milk into the up-turned plunger. Using the plunger as a "wine glass", Alex said, "Cheers" and drank the milk before Kathy could stop him.

Kathy yelled, picked Alex up, and washed out his mouth at the kitchen sink.

She was so worried that she called the "Poison Hotline. When a lady answered, Kathy said, "I don't think you have ever had a question like the one I'm going to ask you."

She said, "Oh Ma'am, I have heard them all."

When Kathy told her what had happened, she laughed and said, "You're right. I've never heard that one before."

She advised Kathy to rinse Alex's mouth with a little mouthwash and he would be okay.

Since neither Kathy nor Fernando drink wine, Alex must have gotten the idea from television.

(It never occurred to me until now that an inverted, toilet-bowl plunger has the shape of a champagne glass."

Alex's Art

♦

(And lost at the beach)

At age four, Alex is drawing pictures with crayons. He likes to draw pictures of his family. He uses a pink crayon to draw Mommy and a black crayon to draw Daddy. When drawing Fernando, he makes sure that his entire face is colored black. (Fernando's complexion is actually dark brown.) Alex never includes Jessica in his family pictures.

One day, at about this time, Fernando took Jessica to the beach to see the Sand Castle Contest. The beach was swarming with people. Fernando bent down to unpack their beach paraphernalia, and Jessica lost sight of him. Believing that they were separated and that she was lost, she looked for a police officer.

When she found an officer, she was crying and she told him she had lost her daddy. When the officer asked what he looked like, she said, "He's a big black man with a dumb hat."

Meanwhile, Fernando had also located a police officer. The two officers established radio contact and reunited the pair.

Dangerous Mission

One day, Fernando and Kathy decided to take the kids fishing at the pier in Imperial Beach, a short drive from Chula Vista and still in the greater San Diego area. Alex was four years old at the time.

There were many people fishing on the pier that day and the Leos family was having a good time.

The lifeguard on the beach, noting that the surfers were getting too close to the fishing pier, announced with a bullhorn, "Surfers, please stay away. You are getting dangerously close to the fishing pier."

In Alex's "world", the announcement translated to, "Persons, stay away. We're going on a dangerous mission on this pier."

Alex was frantic. He kept saying, "We have to go! Didn't you hear the man? They are going on a dangerous mission on this pier."

Although they explained to Alex what the lifeguard had actually said, he would not accept their explanation. It's not what he heard the lifeguard say. He started to cry and he hid under the bench for protection.

Finally, surrendering to Alex's perception of danger, (and to get him to stop crying), the family packed up and returned home. It was a short fishing trip!

(Knowing Alex, as I now do, I'm convinced that he ventures into his own little world from time-to-time. I wonder if other children with ADHD do this?

Kathy says that she would like to be able to visit Alex's special "world" to see what it's like and help her to understand and better cope with his ADHD.)

1994
Alex-Alex-Alex

Alex is now 4 1/2 years old. In a few months, he will be starting kindergarten. Kathy decided that it would be a good idea if he could master the writing of his name before he started school.

After many tries, he was finally able to write "Alex".

Kathy was very proud of his achievement; however, a short time later, she discovered that Alex had decided to autograph everything in the house. The walls, tables, and almost all flat surfaces now bore the name "Alex" in various crayon colors. Even the refrigerator bore his autograph.

Kathy says that later, even though her arms ached from scrubbing off the names, she was still proud of Alex's achievement.

This episode also marked the beginning of the difficult home-teaching assistance that Kathy continues to provide.

Tijuana

As I'm sure most readers know, Tijuana is a sprawling Mexican city just south of San Diego. It is about a thirty-minute drive to the border from the condominium where the Leos family now lived.

The family occasionally drove to Tijuana to have lunch and purchase "Pan Dulce" (sweet bread), a kind of Mexican version of a doughnut.

On one such trip, while waiting to cross the border back to the United States, Alex said "I know why they have 'Police' here."

"Why?" Kathy asked.

"To keep those people in their own country," Alex said.

When they stopped laughing, they informed Alex that they were just leaving his father's birthplace.

Names

One Day, when Jessica was about 5 years old, she asked Kathy where she got the names Jessica and Marie.

Kathy told her that Jessica meant "Gift from God" and that she had seen it in a book of baby names. Marie, Kathy said, was her great grandmother's name. (Actually, it was Maria.)

Alex, who was listening to the conservation, asked, "Where did you get my name, Mama?"

Kathy told him she also found his name in the same book of baby names. "Your first name, 'Alexander', is a Greek name and it means 'Defender of Men', she told him. A man called 'Alexander the Great' was a conqueror of many lands when he was very young. I named you 'James' after your grandfather in Virginia," she told him.

"I thought his name was 'Grandpa'," Alex said.

1996
School

Alex is now five years old and has started kindergarten. Things go well in the beginning; however, a problem soon develops.

Kathy and Fernando decided to move to Virginia. They told the children they would be living in a big house in Virginia with their mother's parents. Alex became very upset upon hearing this. Kathy and Fernando had no idea why.

A possible clue to Alex's anxiety was revealed a short time later in a picture he drew of the Virginia house as he imagined it. It was an older-style, large house with a bell-tower on the roof. It was rather spooky looking, Kathy says.

His anxiety was so bad that he started gagging in class and disrupted the class. Kathy had to pick him up from school nearly every day. Eventually, the school, in frustration, asked Kathy to remove him from kindergarten and restart him in Virginia, and that is what she did.

1997
The Last Move

The Leos family moved to Chesapeake, Virginia shortly after Christmas in January of 1997.

They had celebrated Christmas in Chula Vista at the home of Fernando's parents. Because of the pending move, the children's toys and other gifts were limited; nevertheless, they were satisfied and happy.

*Santa had the foresight to preposition some larger gifts in Chesapeake, so a "second Christmas" would await them.

The children were very surprised when they awoke the first morning in Chesapeake to find so many gifts under the tree that we had left up for their arrival. They wondered why Santa was apparently better to the children in Virginia than to the children in Chula Vista.

When Alex first looked out the window of his upstairs room, he said, "Mama, come look at the big backyard!" He was looking at the wide section of the driveway by the garage entrance. He would think he was in a park later, when he walked into the real backyard: a three-acre lot with over one hundred trees.

*(A later discussion about Santa would cause Alex to throw himself on the bed and exclaim, "This is the worst day of my life."

In School Again

The family settled in quickly in Chesapeake. Fernando got a job at the Naval Base in Norfolk. We were able to provide him a car to get to work. The children were enrolled in local Chesapeake schools.

The first day of school, Alex's teacher said, "We have someone here from California. Who here is from California?"

When no one raised their hand, she asked, "Alex, are you from California?"

"No, I'm from San Diego," Alex replied.

Later, the teacher asked all the students to stand up, one-at-a-time, and recite their three names: first, middle, and last.

Alex raised his hand and said, "I have four names."

After checking the attendance list, the teacher said, "No Alex. You have three names."

"No. I have four."

"Okay. Tell us your four names."

"Alex Zander James Leos."

Alex completed kindergarten without any major problems and has adapted well to his new environment. He loves to play outside in the yard, a major change from the past. His asthma, however, has become more of a problem, probably due to the high pollen count in this area.

Sally and I are enjoying having the family living with us. Fernando has taken over most of the yard work. Kathy helps Sally, and the children are delightful. Some of the following stories about Alex are now my own observation. Kathy's recollections to this point have been, in my opinion, incredible and humorous.

Emergencies

Shortly after Alex started first grade, the school held a fire drill. The teacher explained that some emergencies require the students to leave the school bus and that this had to be done in an orderly manner. They were to practice this drill today, she told them.

When the drill started, the students did as they were told, and got off the bus; all, that is, except Alex.

Alex had leaned forward and tightly grabbed the seat back in front of him and made no move to get off the bus. The teacher asked Alex, "What is the matter?"

"I hate emergencies," Alex said.

The teacher had to pry his hands loose from the seat back.

Sextortion

One day, Alex came home from his first-grade class, dropped his backpack on the kitchen floor, and ran up the stairs to his room. Kathy heard him shaking his piggybank and then saying loudly, "Oh no! I don't have enough!"

Kathy went upstairs to see what he was doing. She noted that he had dumped all his change on the bed. "What are you doing, Alex?"

He said he needed to give an older boy six dollars the next day or the boy would beat him up.

Kathy called the school principal and explained the situation.

The next day, the principal called Alex and the other boy to his office. Alex told his side of the story. The principal then asked the other boy if he had threatened Alex, as Alex had said. According to Alex, the boy said, "He wanted to give me six dollars to beat him up." Whatever he actually said, it was enough to convince the principal that Alex was telling the truth.

The parents of the older boy were called to the school to talk to the principal. Afterwards, their son apologized to Alex.

When Alex came home from school that day, he told Kathy that the boy had said that he got in big trouble because his father said that what he had done to Alex was a crime.

"They call the crime 'Sextortion'," Alex said.

(It sounds like it should be a crime.)

Homework and Study

The advent of school brought considerable, new problems for both Alex and Kathy. Now there was homework, and study for quizzes and tests.

Homework began almost as soon as Alex got home from school. The first problem was determining what the homework assignments were. Often, Alex had only incomplete, scribbled notes, which were meant to outline his homework. Sometimes, a telephone call to the "Homework Hotline"; provided by the school, was required. At other times, a call to a designated, "Study Buddy" was helpful.

The second problem was that the books required were often left in school rather than found in Alex's backpack.

Even when homework assignments were completed, they were often lost, or just not turned-in to the teacher.

Kathy was (and still is) absolutely committed to helping Alex and this was by no means an easy job. He was a study in perpetual motion. While Kathy quizzed him verbally, he would roll on the floor, fidget, play with whatever objects were within reach, tear bits of paper, and walk about the room.

While he no longer rolls on the floor, the other habits remain to this day.

It is incredible, at least to me, that most of the time he gives the correct answers to Kathy's questions. What is perhaps more interesting, Kathy has noted that any attempt to stop his fidgeting, results in the loss of correct answers from him. Even telling him to sit still and pay attention, causes him to lose focus.

When I was writing of Alex's study habits, I recalled a time in my life when I would not talk on the phone, drive, or work on a math problem without a cigarette in my hand. There were many other occasions where I needed that cigarette. I wonder if there is some relationship between that and Alex's antics?

Because Kathy insists on Alex doing his homework: as soon as he gets home from school, and I'm sure she is right to do so, by the time they finish, it is time for dinner or too dark to play outside. His evening play is therefore limited, to some extent, to computer games. Earlier in his life, he didn't like to play outside; now, when he would like to, he has little opportunity.

(It seems to me that children are given way too much homework. I'm sure that I never had as much homework as they have when I was in elementary school (1936-1942). Of course there was no ADHD then either. The good Sisters of St. Francis didn't permit it! Any showing of what we now recognize as ADHD behavior, would receive a quick rebuke from the Sister. I still believe those dedicated nuns were incredible teachers and I'm thankful for the education they gave me. I was pleased to receive a Christmas letter last year from my Third-Grade teacher, Sr. Amadeus. I wonder if the Mayo Clinic knew anything about ADHD in 1936? The clinic was only three, short blocks from the school that I attended. I suspect that they had a different name for it in those days.)

Ambushed

When Alex was seven years old, and in the second grade, he was taken from his regular class three-times-a-week to receive extra help with math and English from a Special Education teacher.

Alex did not like this arrangement because he realized that, with one-on-one instruction, he would need to work harder. Also, I think he may have been embarrassed by being singled out for special assistance.

One day, when he was scheduled to leave class for an English lesson, the Special Education teacher was attending a meeting and did not come for Alex.

Later, while on his way to lunch, Alex saw his Special Education teacher coming down the hall toward him. Alex walked faster, looked down, and avoided making eye contact; however, it didn't work. The teacher spotted him. She grabbed his arm, stopped him and told him that, after lunch, they would have an English lesson.

"You just had to ambush me," Alex said.

"Yes," she said, "But that's making good use of your vocabulary words."

The Soccer Game

When Alex was seven years old, he started playing soccer. During one of his first games, he got the ball and started running toward the goal and he was doing a pretty good job of kicking the ball in front of him. He was heading for the goal unopposed; unfortunately, he was heading for his own goal. The other team was just standing by waiting for him to score a goal for them.

Alex's coach yelled, "Alex, you are going the wrong way."

Alex, hearing the coach, stopped, threw both hands to the top of his head, and turned to run in the other direction.

During the rest of the game, anytime Alex or anyone on his team made an error or missed a shot at the goal, all the parents in the stands threw their hands to the top of their heads just as Alex had done. It reminded me of the "Wave" at an NFL game.

This practice, the Alex "Uh oh", continued throughout the rest of the soccer season.

1998
What Candy?

A few days after Christmas, Alex (age 7) and great-grandson Aren (age 4) were in Janet's room watching cartoons on Janet's TV. They noticed a plastic-tube, candy cane on Janet's dresser. It was filled with miniature candy bars and was a gift to Janet from Jessica. The boys opened the candy cane and ate all the candy bars.

Janet came home and quickly noticed evidence of the misdeed. Candy wrappers littered the floor. She decided to round up the most likely (The usual) suspects.

Alex and Aren were playing in Alex's bedroom when Janet confronted them. She asked if they knew who ate her candy. Alex said, "Hummm, candy? Candy huh. Hummm."

Aren looked up at Alex and said very innocently, "We ate them, didn't we Alex?"

Without hesitation, Alex said, "We thought you were through with them."

Also, about this time, the two candy thieves were making a lot of noise when Aren came into the kitchen crying.

Someone asked him what was wrong. He said, "Grandma told me to close the damn door and I didn't even open the damn door."

1998
Alex in Charge

✦

(Eight years old)

One Sunday morning, as the Leos family was entering church, Alex asked Kathy if he could volunteer to help take care of the small children who are left in the church nursery during Mass. Kathy allowed him to go into the nursery but told him to check with the women working there to find out if they would like his help. When Alex went into the nursery, the rest of the family continued on into the worship area.

About midway through the service, Kathy decided to check on Alex. She opened the nursery door slightly and peeked in. She saw Alex pulling a small shoe out of a toy box. He was saying to a child, "Your shoe does not go in the toy box."

After Mass, Kathy opened the nursery door and said, "Come on Alex. Let's go."

Alex, who was sitting on the floor playing with the one (and only) child, and looking very frustrated, said, "I can't go until his mother comes and gets this boy."

"Where is the nursery worker?"

"There's no one here but me and this little boy."

"How did you get this little boy?"

"After I went into the nursery, a woman came in and asked if I was working in the nursery. I said, 'Yes'. She said, 'Okay, here you go', and she handed me this boy."

Alex said he accepted the child because he thought the nursery workers would join him any minute. When Kathy checked on him, she assumed that the adult worker had stepped out to the restroom.

The nursery was not scheduled to be open that day; however, Alex took charge and he did a good job.

The Highest Authority

During a fifth-grade, history test, one of the questions was: What is the highest authority in the land? The expected answer was, of course, "The Constitution."

Alex's answer, "God", was marked incorrect. This puzzled Alex then, and even now, because he believes God should be above the Constitution.

Alex's answer to this question is indicative of the answers he gives to other questions. His answers may be incorrect, but it's often hard to prove him wrong.

One day, I said to him, "Alex, you're an enigma. Do you know what that means?"

Alex said, "Yes. It means that I'm hard to understand."

I was shocked that he knew the meaning of "enigma" and all the more convinced that my depiction of him was accurate.

Hold the Show for Good Citizen Alex

The morning of Alex's graduation from fifth grade, Kathy said to him, "I'll be there to see you graduate."

"You don't have to go," Alex said, "I'm not getting any awards except a Good Citizen Award."

"That's an important award, and I'll be there to see you receive it."

Kathy went to the ceremony. Many special awards were presented. Finally, they commenced reading the names of those receiving the Good Citizen Award. The list was long because, unless a student got an unsatisfactory conduct grade during the year, they were eligible to receive the award. When the presentations for Alex's class were completed, Alex's name had not been called.

Because all the seats had been taken when Kathy arrived, she was standing at the side where Alex was seated. She looked at Alex who was now slumped in his seat with tears in his eyes.

Kathy immediately approached Alex's teacher and asked why Alex had not received an award. The teacher said she didn't know but she would leave and check her records. When she returned, she said that Alex should have received an award; there were no unsatisfactory grades in his record. She said she would prepare an award for Alex and present it to him later.

"No!" Kathy said. "I want him to receive it now."

Without argument, the teacher quietly advised the principal that she was leaving to prepare an award for a student who had apparently been overlooked. She suggested that, rather than delay the ceremony, he continue with presentations to the next class.

Alex's teacher went to the school office and prepared an award. The principal presented it to Alex with his apologies. (I think Kathy should have received a "Good Parent Award.")

Dinner-Table Quizzes

The evening meal is about the only time that all the household members get together. I have gotten into the habit of asking questions at this meal. I started this practice in an attempt to get everyone into a conversation; particularly, Jessica and Alex.

Whenever possible, I pick subjects that the children are currently studying in school. Other times, I choose subjects from the newspaper or TV that I think may be of interest. Alex seems to enjoy these little quizzes and delights giving a correct answer before his sister.

The short stories that follow are from dinner-table quizzes.

One night, the subject of "Vikings" came up. I don't remember why. I asked, "Where did the Vikings come from?"

The adults at the table usually hold back their answers to give the children the first chance and, of course, to see if they know the answer. Jessica said she didn't have a clue, (A favorite expression of hers). Alex said he was thinking about it. Sometimes, when he thinks he knows the answer but just can't pull it from his head, his hands go to his head in his famous "soccer pose".

After receiving no answer, I finally told them that the Vikings came from Norway and Denmark and that they sailed in "Longboats" to plunder the British Isles and parts of Continental Europe.

Alex looked puzzled when he heard my explanation. "I thought they came from Minnesota," he said.

"Well Alex," I said, "Some of them do; however, they are more apt to play football than to plunder cities or "The Mall of America".

During a conversation about Presidents of the United States, I asked, "Do you know what president married a lady who said that by marrying him she would not have to change her stationery?"

When no one came up with the answer, I said, "It was President Roosevelt. Do you know what his wife's name was?"

"Snuggles?" Alex said.

"Snuggles? How in the world did you come up with that?" I asked.

"Well, wasn't his name Teddy?"

"No Alex. I think you have the wrong Roosevelt. The President was Franklin Delano Roosevelt, and his wife's name was Eleanor Roosevelt, even before she married. She was his cousin. Her stationery had her initials on it, and since her name didn't change, she didn't have to change her stationery."

I couldn't imagine what he was thinking about until a couple of days later when I saw a commercial for "Snuggles" and there was a teddy bear in it.

When talking about the Civil War one evening, I asked Alex if he knew which side Virginia was on during the Civil War.

"Yes," Alex said, "They were on the East-Coast side."

A few days ago, I asked Alex if he knew anything about the Lewis and Clark Expedition.

He said, "Yes."

I asked him, "What was the name of Clark's slave that he took with him on the expedition?"

Alex said, "York."

Then I asked if he could tell me anything about York. Alex said that York was black and that he was large and very strong. The Indians thought he was fully covered with some kind of war paint. They had never seen a black man before, Alex said.

Needless to say, I was surprised and impressed with his answer.

Sometimes when Alex gives a correct, but unexpected answer, others at the table think I may have coaxed him before dinner. The reason for that is a "Con Game" that Alex and I pulled off one evening.

I had read a particularly pithy statement by George Will in an editorial in our local paper. After assuring myself of the accuracy of my understanding, through a couple of "Lookups" in my dictionary, I called Alex back to my bedroom. I explained to him the meaning of Mr. Will's statement and had him practice an explanation of it.

That evening, at dinner, I read the statement (that included some words that no one fully understood) and I asked Alex how he felt about the statement. When Alex gave a very lucid response, all jaws dropped, even one fork, I believe. Kathy was an exception; she had heard Alex practicing his response before dinner.

We, Alex and I, pulled this con one more time before they all caught on.

Janet came into the kitchen the other day asking if anyone had seen her DVD "Finding NEMO".

Alex said, "How ironic, that you can't find NEMO."

Last week, we were talking about the movie, "The Passion of The Christ". Fernando and Alex were planning to see it. Janet asked Alex if he knew a word that we use today that relates to "Crucifixion".

"Excruciating," Alex said.

(My enigma strikes again----------------------twice!)

2003
The Fire Drill

I decided to hold a fire drill. I sleep in a downstairs bedroom. Jessica and Alex have bedrooms upstairs as do Kathy and Fernando, and also Janet. One night, after everyone had gone to sleep, I caused the smoke alarm to sound. After a few seconds, I yelled, "This is a drill. There is a fire in the kitchen."

The actions that followed, justified my concern that the drill was necessary.

No one vacated the house! Janet's room is furthest from the alarm, and she didn't hear it. Alex, true to his earlier, school-bus ("I hate emergencies") drill, sat on the edge of his bed and refused to move.

Needless to say, I was glad we conducted the drill.

Following the drill, we installed battery-operated emergency lights at the top of each stairway and replaced one faulty smoke alarm. Perhaps more importantly, we conducted several, walk-through drills discussing the specific actions to be taken and the different means of egress from the house. Instructions are also given to overnight guests of the children. Kathy is assigned the job of taking Alex in tow to the designated outside area.

Hopefully, we will never have a fire; however, I believe we are now better prepared should that happen.

2004
The Caravan

Jessica had a friend over to dinner the other day. As is her habit, she introduced her friend to me. Her name is Rachel. I told her that Rachel is a nice name, and asked her if she knew the story of Rachel in the Old Testament of the Bible. When she said she didn't, I suggested that she read it, and she said she would. Alex was at the table, and later, when only he and I remained, I asked him if he knew the story of Rachel. He said he didn't.

I told Alex the story of Jacob who, after falling in love with his cousin Rachel, was tricked by her father into marrying Rachel's older sister Lia. After seven more years of working for her father Laban, Jacob was given Rachel to marry.

After many years of having no children, Rachel gave birth to Joseph. Jacob favored Joseph over his brothers, whose mother was Lia. His brothers were jealous of Joseph and decided to kill him. They took him into the desert, and while they were discussing his fate, a caravan of traders came by enroute to Egypt and, rather than kill Joseph, they sold him to the traders in the caravan.

"A Dodge Caravan?" Alex asked.

(Alex could use a little more familiarity with the Bible; couldn't we all.)

Alien Abduction

One balmy, Sunday afternoon, we decided to have dinner on our newly constructed deck in the back yard.

Alex had gone outside to play with his friend across the street. When he left, we were all in the house; some in the kitchen, and others in the den. Alex had been told to return home in about an hour, in time for dinner.

When Alex returned home, we were all on the deck and Alex did not notice us. He looked in every room of the house but never looked on the deck. This was probably the first time he had ever been completely alone in the house.

Since none of us were in the house, all the cars in the driveway, and Alex knew we were preparing dinner, Alex reached the only logical conclusion. Through the open kitchen window, we heard him say in a loud voice, "Oh my God, they have been abducted by aliens!"

(Alex had watched a program about alien abduction the night before.)

2004
Canadians Talk Funny

When I first see Jessica and Alex, in the afternoon when they come home from school, I always ask, "How was school today?" The answer is invariably, "Good" or "Fine". This one-word answer is not restricted to Alex and Jessica; my other grandchildren usually give the same answer.

One day last week, I said to Alex, "I don't understand how school can always he 'Good' or 'Fine'. It seems to me that some days might not be so good; in fact, some might be downright terrible."

The day after I said that, I said to Alex, "How was school today Alex?"

"Not very good. I had an argument with my teacher."

"What about?"

"Well, he kept saying 'futher' instead of 'further'."

"Where is your teacher from? I believe I've heard some southerners pronounce it that way."

"I don't know where he's from. I asked him if he was from Canada. Canadians talk kind of funny, don't they grandpa?"

"No Alex. I don't think Canadians talk funny. You must be thinking of the English. They all talk funny."

(I should bite the Irish half of my tongue.)

"Anyway," Alex said, "My teacher got mad at me and told me to be quiet."

2004
Walking Crooked

Alex usually walks with his head slightly cocked to one side. Apparently, he has done this for years, and we have no explanation of why he does that. I have noticed that he also does this when he runs.

Last Friday, he went on a field trip to participate in a choral contest. The members of the chorus are required to stand very straight when performing. Alex, uncharacteristically, stands very straight when the Director gives the appropriate signal.

The weekend after the choral event, Alex complained of a stiff and sore neck. He kept his head very much cocked to one side, and thought he should be taken to a doctor and fitted for a neck brace.

The following Monday, one of his teachers said to him, "Alex, you seem to be kind of down today. What's the problem?"

"Well, you would be down too if you had to walk around crooked all week-end."

(The only thing this "Crook" stole, was a smile from the teacher when he explained the problem.)

2004
I Hate Hyphens

The evening homework for science included a study of sea life, and in particular, invertebrates. As Kathy looked it over, she noticed the word "TACEANS."

"What is this word 'TACEANS' Alex? I've never heard of it."

"That's because you probably never knew the correct scientific term," Alex said.

"Let me see your book, Alex."

When Kathy looked in the book, she did find the word TACEANS at the far left side of one line. Immediately above that line, on the far right, was the word CRUS-.

When she pointed out to Alex that the correct word was CRUSTACEANS which was joined together by a hyphen, Alex said, "I hate hyphens!"

2004
<u>*Grandpa: The Life Saver*</u>

Alex came back to my bedroom where I was watching TV. He said, "Grandpa, do you have an albuterol inhaler? Mine is empty, and I need one."

I looked in my dresser and located one. I said to Alex, "Here, take this. This is the last one I have though."

Later that evening, when I talked to Kathy, she said; "Alex told me he got your last inhaler. He said I should keep better track of his medicine. 'If it weren't for grandpa, I'd probably die', he said."

6-14-04
Ask for Grandpa

A friend of mine called me today from Tennessee, just to say hello and to check on my health.

Alex answered the phone. When I walked toward the kitchen, Alex had the phone to his ear. I asked Alex who was calling. He asked the caller and then told me. I said, "Okay Alex, I'll take it." When I took the phone, the line was dead.

I quickly called my friend. He said, "Who answered the phone when I called?"

I told him, "My grandson Alex."

"Well when I asked to speak to Jim Brink, he told me that you didn't live there. After I gave him my name, I hung up to recheck your phone number."

"Well Larry, the next time you call, ask to speak to Grandpa; he thinks that's my name."

(Alex has an uncle named Jim Brink and a cousin named Jim Brink; however, my name is, of course, Grandpa.)

June 2004
"ANDER"

Alex's final Report Card for his seventh-grade work arrived. He received one "C"; the rest of his grades were "A's" and "B's". The last two years, I've given him twenty dollars as long as all his grades were "C" or above.

With a twenty-dollar bill in my hand, I called Alex down to the kitchen from his room. "Alex, I've got a very simple question for you and I'll give you this twenty dollars if you answer it correctly. It's really easy. Just spell your middle name."

Alex, very excited, said, "Okay. Just give me a minute A-N-D-E-R."

"What!" I said.

Kathy, who was sitting at the kitchen table, was laughing hysterically. Finally, she said, "Alex! Your middle name is James!"

Alex, hands to his head in his famous soccer pose, said, "Oh my God! I can't believe I said that!"

He was very embarrassed. I said, "Well, I won't tell anyone; I'll just put it in my book."

I gave him the twenty dollars, of course, since it was for his good grades and the effort he put in to get them.

Kathy mentioned later that one of Alex's teachers said that we should call him Alexander more often rather than just "Alex". Maybe she is right.

June 2004
Drinking Causes Trouble

My grandson, David Asbury, invited Jessica and Alex to his house for an eight-grade, end-of-year party. Jessica was in eight grade; Alex was in seventh. No matter, all the children in the family were invited, regardless of grade.

Alex decided not to go. Kathy asked him why. "Someone might get drunk and I don't want to get in trouble."

We don't know where he gets such strange ideas. TV? Perhaps. We think he just didn't want to go and that was the only reason that came to mind at the time.

June 2004
A Police Record?

Alex was in the front yard playing with two neighbor boys. The boys are brothers, ages thirteen and ten.

The three were throwing pinecones at one another. They had made a rule that the face was off-limits as a target. Unfortunately, either on purpose or accidentally, the younger brother hit the older in the face with a pinecone and they started to scuffle. Alex tried to break them up but wasn't having much success. Alex went into the house and told Kathy what was going on.

Someone, who had been walking by and didn't know the boys, noticed the scuffling and the crying, and called the police.

Two police cars quickly showed up and an officer came to the front door to talk to Kathy. After everyone was convinced that the kids were "Just horsing around" as the officer put it, the police left.

Alex was very upset and said, "I suppose I have a police record now."

"No," Kathy said smiling, "I'm the one that has the record for being the mother of a juvenile delinquent."

Motivation, Memories & Missing Notebooks

In 1997, when the Leos family moved in with my wife and me here in Chesapeake, Virginia, I suggested to Kathy that she write down the "Alex Episodes" because someone may want to write a book about him. That someone, after several years and albeit by default, turned out to be me.

I decided to start with Alex's birth and I asked Kathy to check her notes, which she had been recording in a notebook for some time. When she returned from her room, she said her notebook was gone.

"Gone where?" I asked.

"Alex probably took it," she said.

"Why?"

"He probably wanted some scratch paper."

"Should we ask him if he took it?"

"No. It wouldn't do any good. He would just say 'No', 'I don't know', or 'Jessica probably took it'."

Recently, I woke up one morning determined to write more of the "Alex Saga". I asked Kathy to bring me the "new" notebook, the one I purchased when the original could not be located. When she returned to my desk without it, she said, "I think I did a dumb thing."

"What?" I asked.

"Yesterday, I was writing in the notebook at the kitchen table when Alex came home from school. I immediately checked his notebooks, as I always do, to see what homework he needed to do, and then returned them to his backpack. My notebook is probably in Alex's backpack."

I couldn't believe we had lost another notebook. "This can't be happening," I said. "If Alex has it, we will never see that notebook again."

Kathy felt responsible for the loss so she volunteered to go to the school and attempt to retrieve the notebook. "I need to take Jessica some lunch money anyway," she said.

At the school, Kathy requested that they have Alex report to the office with his backpack.

Alex reported as requested. His backpack, however, was empty.

"Did you see my blue notebook in you backpack this morning, Alex?" Kathy asked.

"Yes."

"Well, where is it?"

"In my classroom."

"Why didn't you bring it here to the office?"

"You didn't ask me to. You asked me to bring my backpack."

"Alex! Go back to your classroom and bring me that notebook!"

"Okay, but it's not my fault."

When Alex left, a woman in the office said, "It's a boy thing."

"No," Kathy said, "It's an ADHD thing."

"Oh, then you have double trouble," she said.

"Yes, but also double Pride and Joy."

The notebook is still here, resting on a table in the dining room. New stories are being added, but we must stop this writing sometime. God willing, Alex will continue to provide stories for many years to come. I hope someone will write them down.

August 2004
"Don't Act Stupid"

Summer is almost over and school will be starting in about two weeks. Jessica will be in ninth grade and Alex in eight.

This morning, quite early, one of Alex's friends rang the doorbell. The lad seemed to be quite upset and he asked to see Alex. I had him come in and I called upstairs for Alex. Alex got up, and while he was dressing, I talked to the boy.

He said he was having an argument with his mother. She wanted him to take medicine for his ADHD but he didn't want to take it. I got the impression that he had been off the medicine for awhile.

Kathy told me later that some parents take their children off the ADHD medicine during the summer. Then, about two weeks before the start of school, they restart the medicine. Kathy said she didn't think this was a good idea, and I don't know if this was the cause of the visiting boy's distress. I believe the boy sought out Alex as someone who would understand his problem because he knew Alex also has ADHD.

Alex came downstairs and he and friend went up to Alex's room. Kathy, who was in the kitchen then, overheard Alex giving his friend the following advice:

"You have to tell your mom how you feel. She thinks you are just acting stupid and you can't help it, so you need medication. I understand how medication can make you feel 'zoney' because it makes me feel that way too. It also makes me feel sick to my stomach. That's why I don't take it anymore. I don't have any problem because people around here understand how I am. You just have to try to control yourself and not act stupid."

Neighborhood Politics

Alex was across the street playing with his friend. His friend's parents asked both of them to come in by the TV and watch a little of the Republican Convention. Alex only watched for a short time. When he came home, he said, "I was watching those Republicans and I got madder and madder listening to those idiots talk."

I didn't realize Alex was even interested in politics but Kathy said that Alex and his friend often argue about politics. She said that one day, his friend jumped on Alex from behind and Alex quickly flipped him over onto his back. Alex told him, "You're just like Bush. You jump before you think."

Kathy was reminded of what Alex once said when he was seven: Mama, are we Republicans or "DemoCRAPS?"

Epilogue

Alexander James Leos is now thirteen. He is 5 feet 4 inches tall and he weighs 145 pounds. He is Hispanic looking and has thick, black hair. He is stocky, nice looking, and very photogenic. He is incredibly strong for his age. He has not outgrown his chronic asthma and sometimes suffers severe attacks. It is therefore necessary to have inhalers available wherever he may be.

Alex is in seventh grade. Generally, he does quite well in school. His mother, Kathy, still works with him nearly every evening. His favorite subjects seem to be history and science. He has some difficulty with English, and he receives extra help with math. He often makes the Honor Roll. In fact, he has done so recently and I have enclosed a copy of his recent grades.

He is still the object of some teasing and taunting from schoolmates; however, those who have pushed him too far and underestimated his response and strength have learned a painful lesson. Lately, we have cautioned him to refrain from physical response, insofar as possible, for fear that, because of his superior strength, he could seriously hurt someone. We have never known him to initiate a fight and he is very good to little children.

As I review the pages I have written, I feel the need to repeat, or clarify, a couple of points. First, Alex is not a clown; the humorous things that he does are not planned. Secondly, Alex is not stupid; he merely has a learning disability. Those of you who have an interest in history, know that many great men and women had learning disabilities. Whether Alex ever becomes a recognized great man remains to be seen. We are satisfied at this time that he is a great son and a great (though enigmatic) grandson.

CHESAPEAKE PUBLIC SCHOOLS

✦

Official Grade Report

Hickory Middle School

2003-2004

Student—Alexander Leos

Course	01 Semester	02 Semester	03 Semester	04 Semester	Final Grade
English 7	A	A	B	B	A
Chorus 7	A	A	A	A	A
U S History	B	B	B	B	B
Life Science 7	B	B	A	B	B
ACSUP Math	C	C	C	C	C
PE/Health 7	A	B	B	C	B

978-0-595-34901-2
0-595-34901-3